Reflections of
New Zealand

A Hum

firstpic® photographers

Helicopters offer a completely different
perspective of Central Otago and the
Southern Alps, not to mention a great
way to get to the tops for a ski lane
all on your own.

Southern Alps, Central Otago.

Lake views from every room...
The Church of the Good Shepherd
sits on the shore of Lake Tekapo.
Built in stone by the first
missionaries to arrive from
Great Britain, it serves as a solid
reminder of their Scottish heritage.

Church of the Good Shepherd, Lake Tekapo.

Once wild, then farmed and now wild once more. Early settlers introduced deer and thar, primarily for sport. They also took up farming leases in the South Island high country but now the 'tops' are classified as "Class 8" country and many areas are now closed for grazing. Deer are now farmed on the low lands.

High country, Central Otago.

Washday perhaps?

This unusual bra fence near Wanaka at the southern end of the Crown Range, leaves many a traveller agape.

Amusing surprises await the observant on highways and byways.

Keep an eye out...

Cardrona Valley, Wanaka.

The Cardrona Hotel, on the road over the Crown Range separating Wanaka and Queenstown, is allegedly the home of the true 'southern man'.

The old pub, a popular haunt in goldrush days, remains a welcome road stop for winter sports enthusiasts, travelling down from the Triple Cone Skifields.

Cardrona Valley, Central Otago.

It is possible to really get away from it all in the South Island – this hut at the edge of Mt Cook National Park, is the holiday getaway of overseas owners.

Central Otago and Queenstown is home away from home for a number of overseas movie stars and famous folk, due in part to the heightened international profile brought by The Lord of the Rings trilogy.

Mt Aspiring National Park, Central Otago.

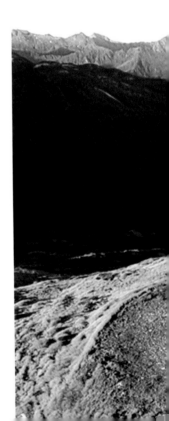

Despite greatly reduced numbers since the 1980s, there are still more sheep than people in New Zealand.

Brought by Captain Cook in 1773, the first sheep to set foot on New Zealand soil were a merino pair which did not survive. Missionary Samuel Marsden's small 1814 Bay of Islands flock did survive, but sheep farming really only began with the establishment of a merino farm on Mana Island, Wellington, in 1834.

Total sheep in 1981 swelled to 70 million, but have fallen since, and now number around 47 million.

Makaroa, Haast Pass.

Remains of the old stone
cottages built by early settlers
can often be seen along roadsides
throughout Central Otago.
Relics and remains of early
Chinese goldmining settlements
can sometimes be found.

Glenorchy, Central Otago.

Leaf change in the South Island
is spectacular, when with the
first chill of winter, poplar,
liquid amber, oak, elm and
ash turn brilliant hues.

Wanaka.

Hills rise steeply from
the flats along the upper
West Coast of the South Island.
Dirt roads heading seemingly
into nowhere draw the
curious traveller on.

West Coast, South Island.

THE BOAT SHED
CAFE · BAR · RESTAURANT

Winner of Nelson Best Restaurant 2001 · 2002 · 2003

Nelson is New Zealand's largest fishing port and a producer of a bounty of fruits and vegetables as well as hops. It has many restaurants, vineyards and boutique breweries to tempt the traveller.

Nelson.

Harnessing the wind for power is not a new concept but one that is being increasingly considered as an alternative to fossil fuel power generation.

Tararua Range, Wellington.

Many farmers in New Zealand
spend their days working amidst
some of the most beautiful scenery
imaginable, their only companions
their faithful working dogs.
Many continue to farm land which has
been in their families for generations.

Parakino, Wanganui River.

Mt Taranaki (or Mt Egmont as it was named by Captain Cook), is said to not always have been sited in central Taranaki. According to Maori legend, Taranaki was long ago at the centre of the North Island, along with Ruapaehu, Tongariro, Nguarahoe, Tauhara and Putauaki, all of whom were male and all in love with tree-clad female mountain Pihanga.

Taranaki and Tongariro fought, with Tongariro emerging as victor. Taranaki was driven away, cutting a deep trough to the south, which became the Wanganui River. The sorrows of Taranaki at the loss of his love, Pihanga, are represented by the clouds that so often cloak the mountain's peak.

Mt Taranaki, Taranaki.

It's still possible in New Zealand
to be pleasantly surprised by
small mobs of sheep or cattle
on the move on quiet back
country roads.

Gisborne.

Corrugated iron is almost a New Zealand icon.

It serves as everything from a trusty roofing material to the

cladding on sheds and barns.
Resourceful country folk even
use iron to fashion letterboxes
and old appliances are
reincarnated as post boxes!

East Coast and Far North.

Take time out to admire the
fine carving commemorating
the Anzac soldiers who fell in
World War II at the Hinemahuru
Marae on the East Coast.

The Anzac Gate, the work of local
carvers, depicts members of the
Maori Battalion, many of whom
came from this area.

Raukokore, East Coast.

The old NZ Shipping Company building at Tokomaru Bay harks back
to the days when meat and wool from the large sheep farms of the
Gisborne region was shipped direct from the East Coast to British
markets, rather than by the difficult road route to Tauranga.

Tokomaru Bay, East Coast.

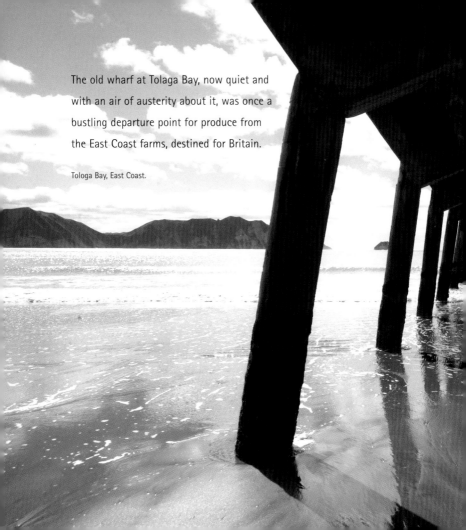

The old wharf at Tolaga Bay, now quiet and with an air of austerity about it, was once a bustling departure point for produce from the East Coast farms, destined for Britain.

Tolaga Bay, East Coast.

The early forests of New Zealand provided vital timbers
for the building of bridges, wharves and dwellings.
No longer in use, nature now stakes her claim,
reminding us that we are just passing by.

Tokomaru Bay, East Coast.

All over New Zealand, even in the most isolated of places, churches of many denominations stand in readiness for their congregations. From the many beautiful Catholic churches of the Hokianga, the distinctive Ratana churches of Wanganui and the Far North to the solid stone churches of Central Otago, each has its story to tell.

Christ Church of Raukokore, East Coast and Church at Pawarenga, North Hokianga.

Old farm cottages which
still dot rural New Zealand,
once provided welcome
warmth and roof for many
a shepherd and shearer.

Coromandel.

It's aptly known as the City of Sails, and on a
clear day, the Waitemata Harbour surrounding
Auckland City is filled with sail boats.
Races and events in and around the
harbour and the Viaduct Basin, home to
past America's Cup challenges, take up
many an Aucklander's weekend.

Waitemata Harbour, Auckland.

City lights merge in the motorway junctions in central Auckland, while the Skytower atop the casino casts its light over all.

Auckland.

From the top of Mt Eden, one of Auckland's 48 volcanic cones,
the city spreads out in every direction. Named Tamaki Makau Rau
by Maori, this multi-cultural city is home to over 1.3 million people.
Over 50 islands make up the Hauraki Gulf, and with many beaches
within an easy drive, it's easy to see why this is the home of
choice for one third of New Zealanders.

Mt Eden, Auckland.

The dramatic coastal scenery at Piha, on Auckland's West Coast, has been immortalised in film and television. But for locals it remains a special place to walk or fish or simply stand and wonder at the power of the sea.

Piha, West Coast.

The most popular comfort stop in the country must surely be the Hundertwasser toilets of Kawakawa.

This unique legacy, attracting thousands of tourists each year, was created by Austrian born artist, designer and environmentalist Frederick Hundertwasser, who made the area his home.

Kawakawa, Bay of Islands.

The historic Waitangi Treaty Grounds in
the Bay of Islands, mark the spot where
the Treaty of Waitangi was signed between
Maori and British, bringing New Zealand
under British rule.

From neighbouring Paihia, it's a short ferry
trip across the bay to Kororareka, or Russell,
where many of the houses, hotels and
shops date back to the whaling days
of the early 1800s.

Treaty Grounds, Waitangi, Bay of Islands.

Te Ohonga, meaning 'awakening' is a whare wananga,
or place of well being, its purpose to awaken people by
guiding them through knowledge and understanding.

Kaitaia.

Once a trusty mode of transport,
now simply part of the scenery.
The humble fisherman's dinghy,
its name implying a far away
Mediterranean significance,
lies in wait for an owner's return.

Pukenui, Far North.

Morning light on the water.
Fishing trawlers, deep sea game fishing
charters and weekend launches use Pukenui
Wharf, on the sheltered Houhora Harbour,
as take off point for journeys out around
the Three Kings Islands and further afield.
Marlin, kingfish, tuna, snapper and crayfish are
unloaded here and trucked out on the first stage
of their journey to local and export markets.

Houhora Harbour, Far North.

Here the two great oceans meet from opposite directions –
the Tasman from the west and the Pacific from the east.

Cape Reinga at New Zealand's northern-most tip is a sacred place for Maori.
This is the departure point of the spirits of the dead, signifying their return to the
mythical homeland of Hawaiiki. Spirits are said to slide down the most northern-most
pohutukawa on the cliff face, into the underworld guarded by Hine te Po.

Cape Reinga, Far North.

Natural forces, even when harnessed for mankind's
purpose, have a beauty all of their own.

Avemore Dam, Waitaki River, Otago.